LET'S GO SIG IN JAPAN!

Learning Geography
Children's Explore the World Books

BABY PROFESSOR
EDUCATION KIDS

Speedy Publishing LLC
40 E. Main St. #1156
Newark, DE 19711
www.speedypublishing.com
Copyright 2017

Japan is an island nation located in East Asia and is surrounded by the Sea of Japan (the East Sea) on one side and the Pacific Ocean on the other side. In this book, we will be learning about what to see when visiting this magnificent country.

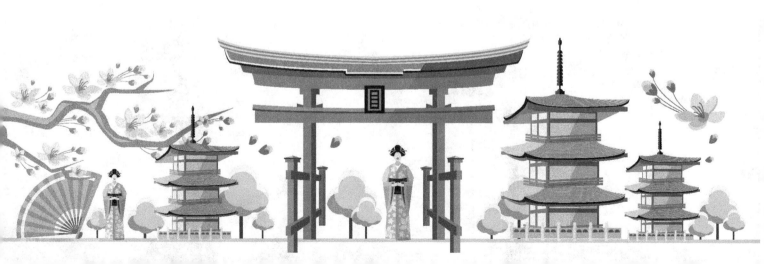

TOKYO

Tokyo is the capital of Japan and is the most populated metropolis in the world. In addition, it is one of Japan's 47 prefectures, that consist of 23 central city wards as well as multiple towns, cities, and villages located west of the city center. The Ogasawara Islands and the Izu Islands are also part of Tokyo.

TOKUGAWA IEYASU

Tokyo was referred to as Edo prior to 1868. As a small castle town of the 16th century, Edo became the political center of Japan in 1603 once Tokugawa Leyasu had established his feudal government there. After a few decades, Edo grew into one of the most populated cities in the world.

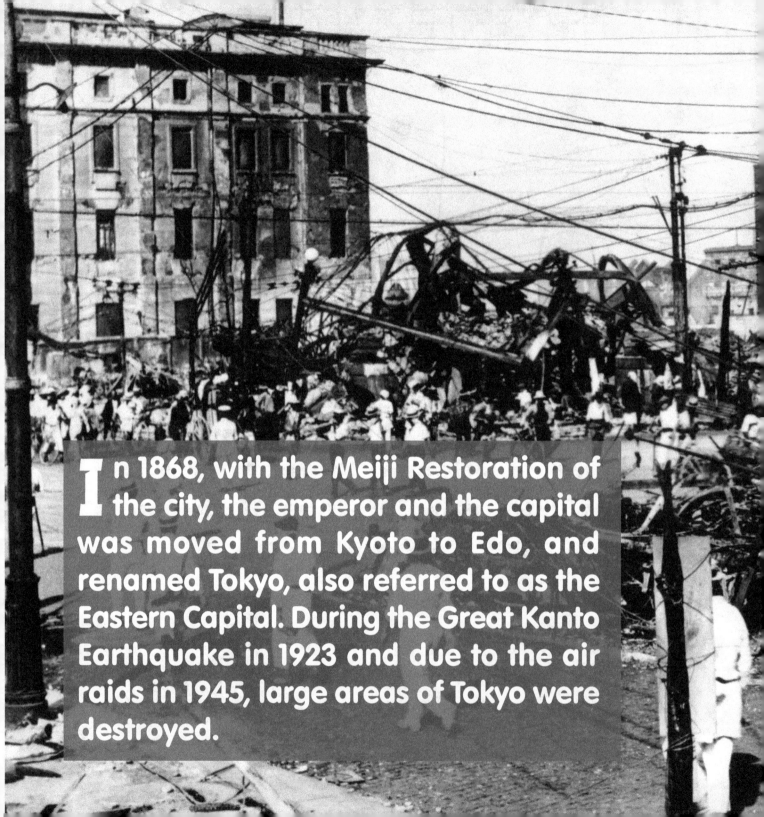

In 1868, with the Meiji Restoration of the city, the emperor and the capital was moved from Kyoto to Edo, and renamed Tokyo, also referred to as the Eastern Capital. During the Great Kanto Earthquake in 1923 and due to the air raids in 1945, large areas of Tokyo were destroyed.

THE GREAT KANTO EARTHQUAKE

ASAKUSA KANNON TEMPLE

Tokyo now offers an unlimited amount of entertainment, dining, culture, and shopping to its visitors. Its history can be appreciated in its districts, including Asakusa, and in its many gardens, historic temples, and excellent museums. It also offers several attractive green spaces located within its city center as well as within short train rides to its outskirts.

THE TOKYO TOWER

Located in the center of Tokyo, the Tokyo Tower stands at 333 meters high. It is known as the tallest, self-supported tower in the world and is 13 meters higher than the Eiffel Tower which is located in Paris, France. As a symbol of the rebirth of Japan's major economic power after the war, the Tower was its tallest structure from 1958, when it was completed, until 2012, when the Tokyo Skytree surpassed it. As well as being a great tourist spot, it also serves as a broadcast antenna.

TOKYO TOWER

Its main observatory is located at 150 meters and can be reached either by elevator or by its 600-step stairway, for which both there is a fee. Because of its central location, the observatory offers a great view of the city, even though it is only located at a moderate height. There are some "look-down windows" built into the floor which you can stand on to look down, a café where you can enjoy some refreshments, as well as a souvenir shop.

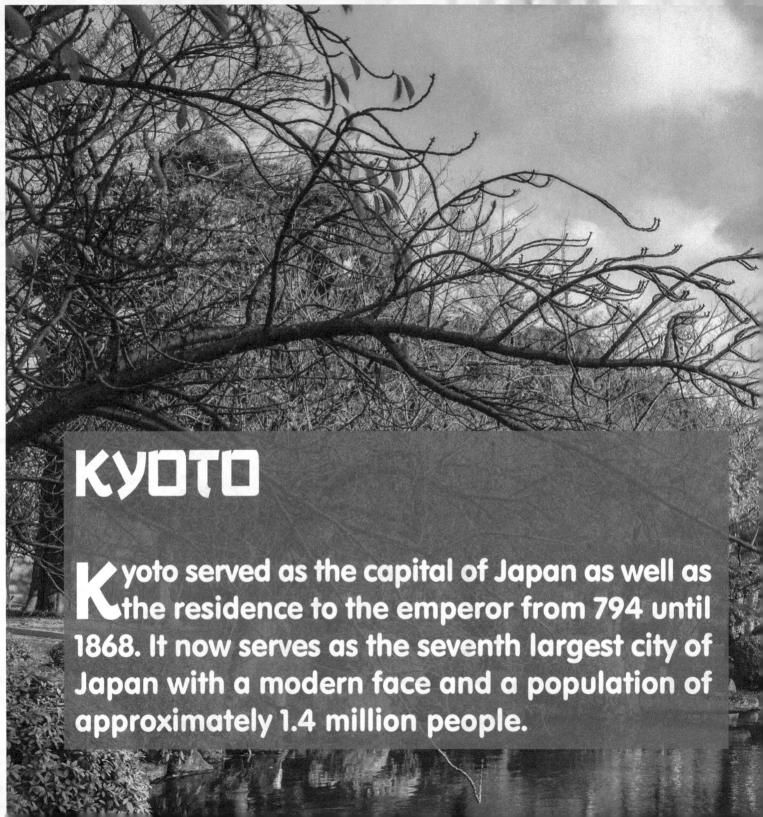

KYOTO

Kyoto served as the capital of Japan as well as the residence to the emperor from 794 until 1868. It now serves as the seventh largest city of Japan with a modern face and a population of approximately 1.4 million people.

WOODEN PAGODA OF TOJI TEMPLE, KYOTO JAPAN

MAIN GATE OF FUSHIMI INARI-TAISHA
SHRINE IN KYOTO

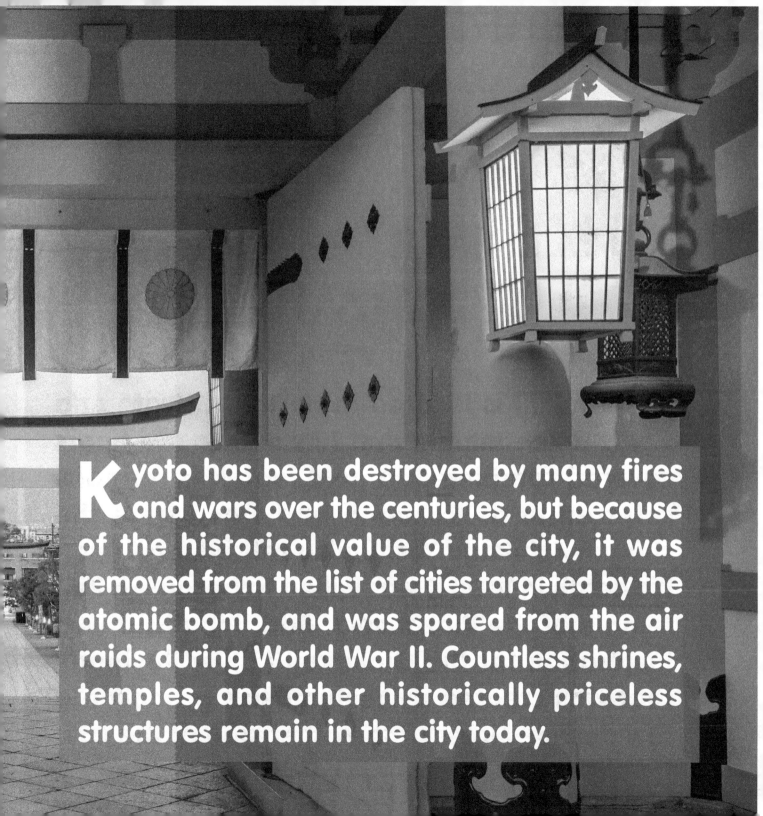

Kyoto has been destroyed by many fires and wars over the centuries, but because of the historical value of the city, it was removed from the list of cities targeted by the atomic bomb, and was spared from the air raids during World War II. Countless shrines, temples, and other historically priceless structures remain in the city today.

KINKAKUJI (GOLDEN PAVILION)

Kinkakuji is located in northern Kyoto and is a Zen temple that has its two top floors covered completed in gold leaf. It is formally referred to as Rokuonji and was where the shogun Ashikaga Yoshimitsu retired, and upon his death in 1408 it was willed to become a Zen temple of the Rinzai sect. Additionally, it was inspiration for the Ginkakuji (Silver Pavilion), that was created by Yoshimitsu's grandson a few decades later at the other side of the city.

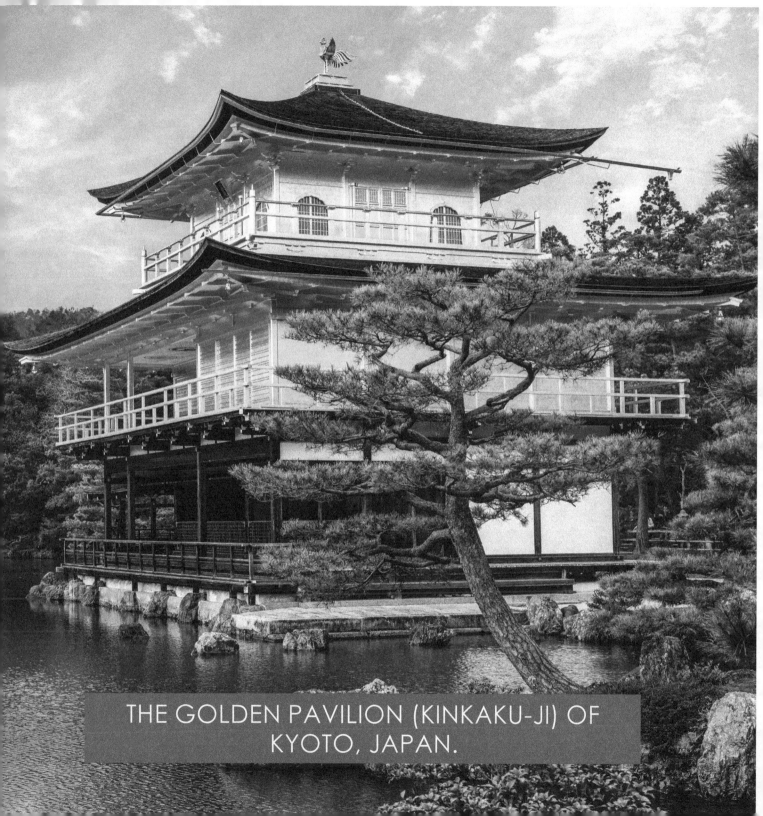

THE GOLDEN PAVILION (KINKAKU-JI) OF KYOTO, JAPAN.

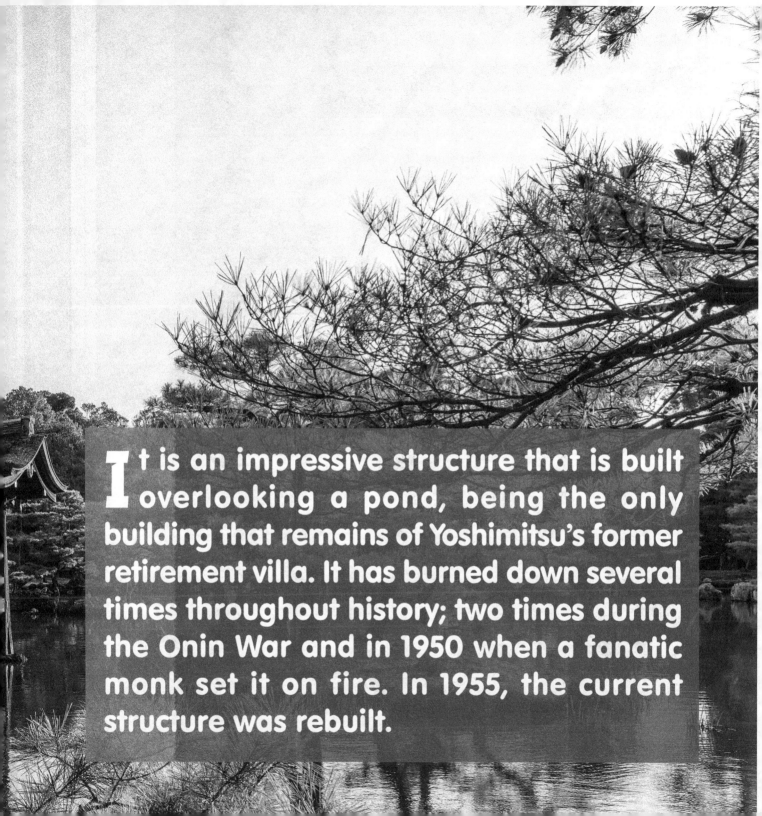

It is an impressive structure that is built overlooking a pond, being the only building that remains of Yoshimitsu's former retirement villa. It has burned down several times throughout history; two times during the Onin War and in 1950 when a fanatic monk set it on fire. In 1955, the current structure was rebuilt.

OSAKA BAY, OSAKA JAPAN

OSAKA

Osaka falls behind Tokyo, being the second largest metropolitan area in Japan. For many centuries, Osaka has been the economic powerhouse of the Kansai region. Previously known as Naniwa, it was once the capital of Japan, prior to the Nara period. This was a time when they would move the capital with each new emperor's reign. Naniwa was the first capital of Japan.

OSAKA CASTLE WITH CHERRY BLOSSOM

Toyotomi Hideyoshi chose Osaka as the location for his castle in the 16th century, and it may have been Japan's political capital if Leyasu had not ended the lineage of Toyotomi after the death of Hideyoshi and relocated his government to Edo, which is now known as Tokyo.

UNIVERSAL STUDIOS JAPAN

Universal Studios Japan was the first Universal Studios brand theme park in Asia. It opened March 2001 located in the Osaka Bay Area, and occupies 39 hectares and has become Japan's most visited amusement park following the Tokyo Disney Resort.

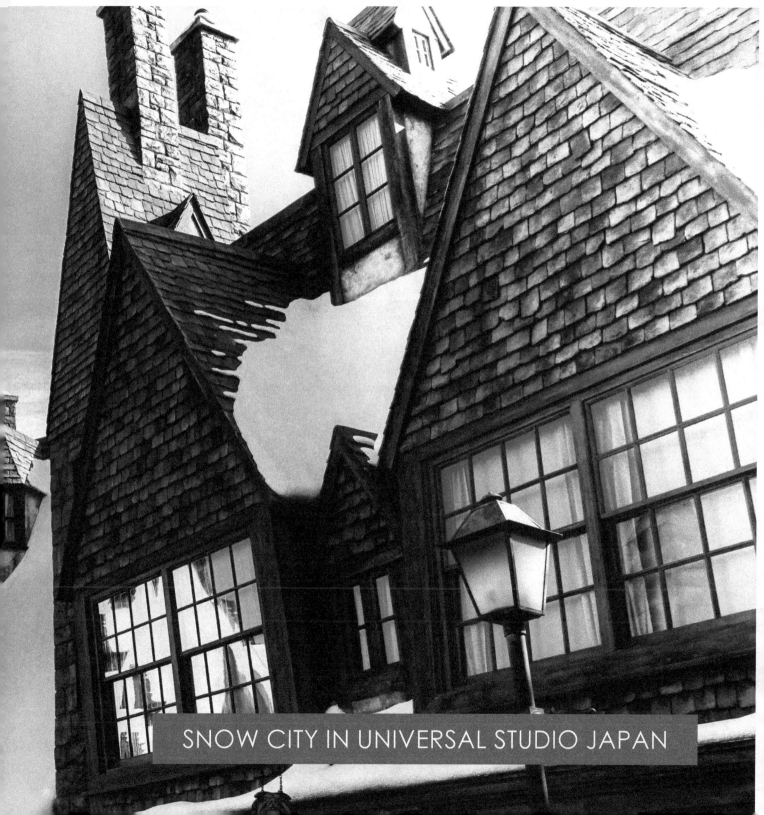
SNOW CITY IN UNIVERSAL STUDIO JAPAN

VIEW OF HOGWARTS

This park offers eight sections: New York, Hollywood, Jurassic Park, San Francisco, Waterworld, Universal Wonderland, Amity Village, as well as The Wizarding World of Harry Potter.

you can also enjoy several amusement rides that range from the child-friendly carousels to the roller coasters and simulators that are based on popular movies that include Jurassic Park, Terminator 2, Back to the Future, and Spiderman.

PARK IN NARA JAPAN

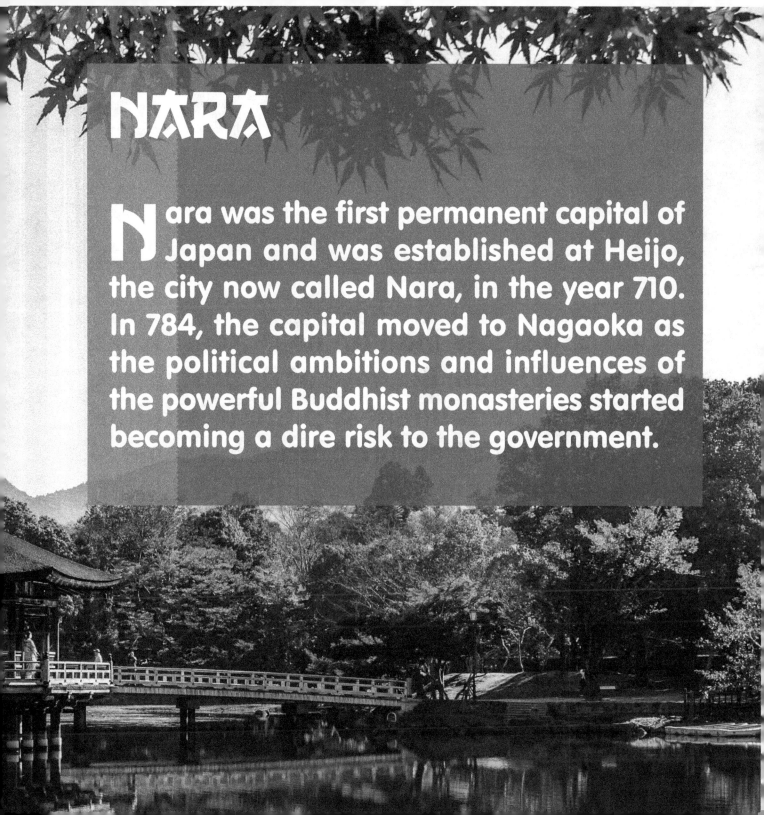

NARA

Nara was the first permanent capital of Japan and was established at Heijo, the city now called Nara, in the year 710. In 784, the capital moved to Nagaoka as the political ambitions and influences of the powerful Buddhist monasteries started becoming a dire risk to the government.

Nara is less than an hour from Osaka and Kyoto. Because of its past, being the first permanent capital, it is full of great historic treasures, including some of the largest and oldest temples in Japan.

A HUGE BUDDHA STATUE IN YAKUSHI-JI TEMPLE IN NARA, JAPAN.

WOODEN MAIN BUILDING OF
TODAIJI TEMPLE IN NARA, JAPAN

THE TODAIJI TEMPLE

Also referred to as the "Great Eastern Temple, the Todaiji Temple is known as a Nara landmark. It is one of Japan's historically significant and most famous temples.

Constructed in the year 752, this temple was created as the head of all of Japan's provincial Buddhist temples and grew so rapidly that in 784 they moved the capital to Nagaoka so as to lower its influence on governmental affairs.

虚空蔵

MIYAJIMA, HIROSHIMA, JAPAN AT THE
FLOATING GATE OF ITSUKUSHIMA SHRINE.

HIROSHIMA

Hiroshima is the main city of the Chugoku Region and is home to more than a million people.

On August 6, 1945, when the first atomic bomb was dropped over it, Hiroshima became known around the world for this unenviable distinction. Its destructive power was massive and almost eradicated everything located within a two-kilometer radius.

ATOMIC BOMB DOME MEMORIAL BUILDING
IN HIROSHIMA, JAPAN

HIROSHIMA CASTLE ON THE SIDE OF
OTAGAWA RIVER IN AUTUMN

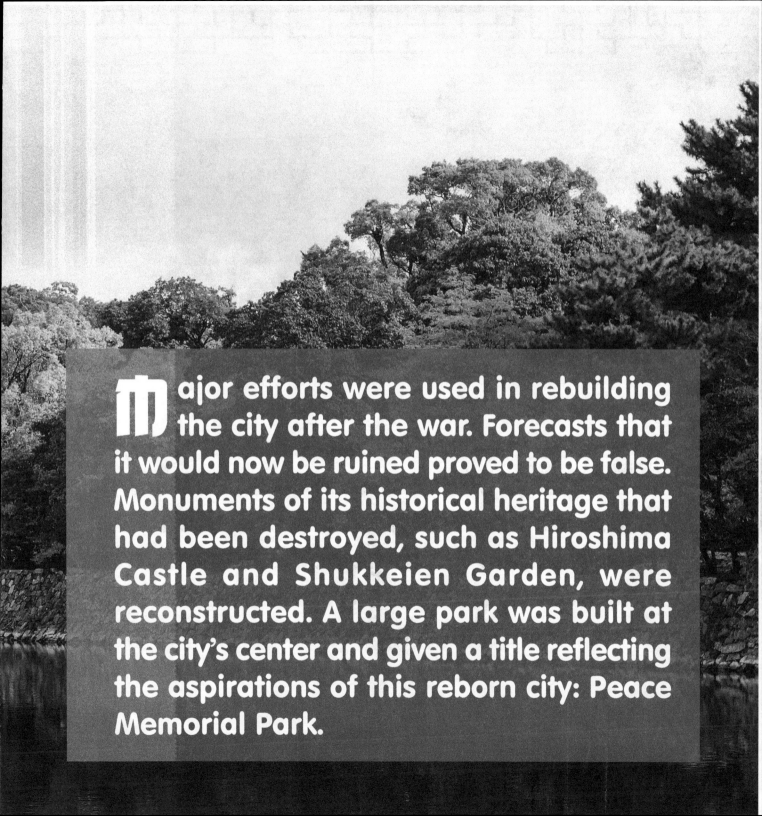

Major efforts were used in rebuilding the city after the war. Forecasts that it would now be ruined proved to be false. Monuments of its historical heritage that had been destroyed, such as Hiroshima Castle and Shukkeien Garden, were reconstructed. A large park was built at the city's center and given a title reflecting the aspirations of this reborn city: Peace Memorial Park.

PEACE MEMORIAL PARK

Peace Memorial Park is one of the city's most prominent features. Visitors not even looking for it will more than likely stumble upon this large park. Its lawns, trees, and walking paths are a stark contrast to the surrounding area of downtown Hiroshima.

HIROSHIMA PEACE MEMORIAL PARK

Prior to the bombing, the area now known as Peace Park had been the commercial and political heart of Hiroshima and that was why it became the pilot's target. It was decided four years to the day after the bomb had been dropped that it would not be redeveloped but rather devoted to peace memorial facilities.

MOUNT FUJI

At 3,776 meters, Mount Fuji is Japan's highest mountain, and not surprisingly, this almost perfectly shaped volcano has been worshipped as sacred and has been largely popular among common people and artists for centuries.

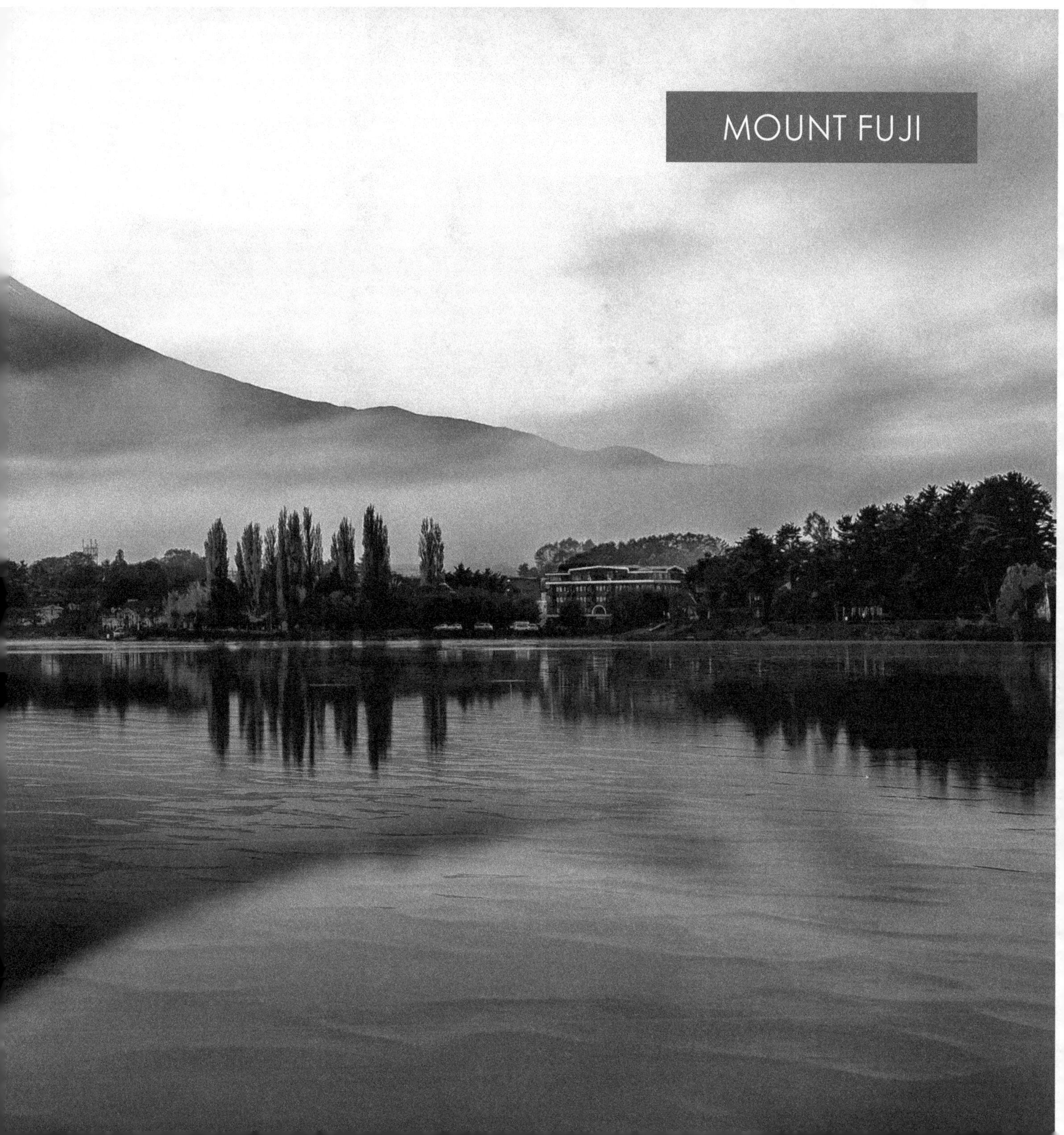
MOUNT FUJI

Mount Fuji is considered to be an active volcano, and its most recent eruption occurred in 1707. It is located between Shizuoka and Yamanashi Prefectures, on the border, and on clear days can be viewed from Yokohama and Tokyo.

Another simple way to enjoy the view of Mount Fuji is to take the train between Osaka and Tokyo. For the best view, take the train from Tokyo towards Nagoya, Kyoto, and Osaka and at the Shin-Fuji station, about 40-45 minutes into your journey, look towards the right-hand side of the train.

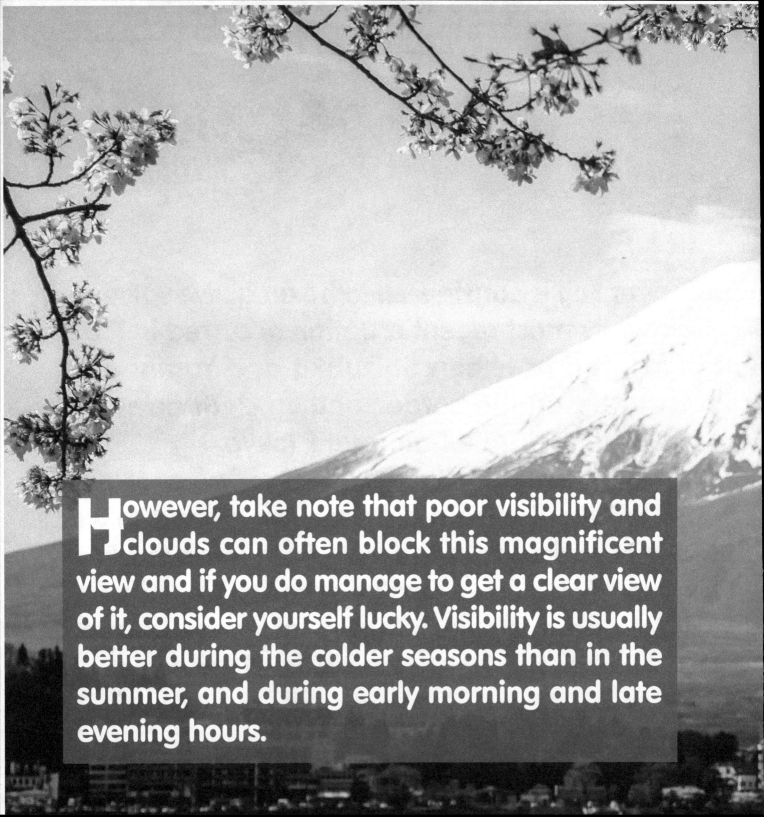

However, take note that poor visibility and clouds can often block this magnificent view and if you do manage to get a clear view of it, consider yourself lucky. Visibility is usually better during the colder seasons than in the summer, and during early morning and late evening hours.

OWAKUDANI HOT SPRING AREA NEAR
LAKE ASHI IN HAKONE, JAPAN

If you would like to enjoy it to a slower pace and from a natural surrounding you might want to go to Fujigoko (the Fuji Five Lake) region located at the north foot of the mountain, or you might enjoy going to Hakone, which is a hot spring resort. For the more adventurous person, Mount Fuji officially opens for climbing in July and August.

**T**here are so many other famous places to visit in Japan. Japan is known for its architecture and its gardens as well.

For additional information about Japan, you can go to your local library, research the internet, and ask questions of your teachers, family, and friends.

Visit

BABY PROFESSOR
EDUCATION KIDS

www.BabyProfessorBooks.com
to download Free Baby Professor eBooks
and view our catalog of new and exciting
Children's Books

CPSIA information can be obtained
at www.ICGtesting.com
Printed in the USA
LVHW061943050922
727603LV00037B/810